Love Pane

Open your inner window, release your feelings and heal through Haiku; a simple but powerful form of creative expression.

By Stella Shen

This book is a work of fiction. All names, characters, places and incidents are the product of the author's imagination, and any resemblance to actual events, locales or persons is entirely coincidental.

First printing: July, 2008
Second printing: February, 2010
Third printing: March, 2015

The haiku poems 'The Spring Night', 'They Come Out', 'Stillness', 'Harvest Moon', and 'Winter Moon' are translated by William J. Higginson from Japanese classics. They are featured in his book 'Butterfly Dreams: The Seasons through Haiku and Photographs', with photographs by Michael Lustbader (published by Natural Tapestries Publishing, copyright © 2006 by William J. Higginson). Reproduced here by the kind permission of the translator.

For Ethan

moonlight...

my boy's twinkling laughter

steals my heart

Contents

Chapter One – Haiku, an Introduction

If you are in pain due to love, bereavement, uncertainty, worry or any other difficult aspect of your reality, you can take control and self-heal. Using your own words you can express your pain or your hopes. Expression through poetry is a recognised way of coping with stress or unhappiness; poetry can be used as a message of happiness and hope. The style of poetry offered to you here is the haiku. Haiku is ideal for self-healing. Uncover the history, spirit and rules of haiku and you will have a powerful tool in your hands for your own healing.

This guide answers three questions: What is haiku? How do I write haiku? How can I heal through haiku? Here is a brief introduction of what this guide will cover.

What is Haiku?
Haiku is a form of Japanese poetry known for its simplicity of structure and its language of images. There were four great Haiku Masters; the last, Masaoka Shiki (1867-1902), established modern haiku as a new independent poetic form. The haiku spirit is vital to the haiku and has been passed down through the ages. This spirit encourages the shedding of a fresh light on everyday situations, a focus on the 'now', along with a close interaction with nature.

How do I write Haiku?
Haiku follows varying rules to different degrees of strictness. For those who want a very clear structure, following all or the majority of the rules of haiku will provide this. Haiku-poems also lend themselves to the development of individual style. This may be more suitable for those who wish to follow the rules with more flexibility or to focus on one or two rules only. One of the reasons that haiku is so well suited to self-healing is that it gives you the freedom to express yourself in the way in which you choose, but still within the guidelines of the genre. In this guide you will be introduced to the eight main rules of haiku.

How do I heal through Haiku?

Haiku is a truly excellent tool for self-healing for many reasons. Its simplicity makes it an accessible form of creative expression and its focus on the 'now' encourages you to suspend your thoughts about the past and the future and focus on the present moment. The role of nature in haiku gives you the opportunity to observe and to experience its beauty and harmony. Immersing yourself in nature and interacting with beauty and harmony will have healing benefits. You can also use your haiku as a way to communicate with others in either a direct or indirect way, depending on your choice. Through haiku you can tell them about your feelings and any situation that you are experiencing.

When writing your haiku, there are various techniques that you can use to work through your healing step-by-step. You may be going through something very painful or unsettling in your life such as bereavement, the breakdown of a relationship or redundancy. Such situations may have a profound effect on you and you may find yourself experiencing different emotions such as denial, anger and depression. We will look more closely at these different emotions and offer you three techniques designed to help you work through these to ultimately reach a point of acceptance and change. The three techniques describe the three steps of:

- reflecting upon your feelings,
- expressing your feelings, and
- acknowledging your feelings.

For each technique there are instructions on how to write the haiku.

We will explore the three techniques further with examples later on in the guide. You will no doubt develop and create your own techniques too. The three techniques offered here are, in brief:

Technique One - Examine your current feelings

Reflect upon your feelings. Use your haiku to coax your feelings into your conscious mind. Use your haiku to explore what you are feeling and why.

Technique Two – Express your feelings through symbolism

Express your feelings. Use your haiku as a way to express and let out your feelings in a less direct way.

Technique Three – Acknowledge your feelings

Acknowledge your feelings. Use your haiku to describe in a direct way what your feelings are. Empower yourself to look at these feelings and to release them. Let go of aspects of your reality that have a negative impact on you.

These are essential steps in being able to deal with your feelings and bring about any change that you want for yourself or for your life. At any time during these techniques, you can create your own affirming haiku. This will help the healing process as you are in control of projecting what you want to feel and what you want to experience. We will also cover how to write an affirming haiku.

Chapter Two – The Heart of Haiku

What is Haiku? The History and Spirit of Haiku

Haiku is an important form of Japanese poetry characterised by its simplicity of structure and its rich medium of images. This simplicity of structure makes the haiku an accessible form of creative expression without the complexity of Western poetry. Modern haiku was established as a new independent poetic form by Masaoka Shiki, the last of the Four Great Haiku Masters. The Four Great Haiku Masters were Matsuo Bashô (1644-1694), Yosa Buson (1716-1784), Kobayashi Issa (1762-1826) and Masaoka Shiki (1867-1902). Some of their work can be seen later on in this guide. The haiku spirit is vital to the haiku and has been passed down through the ages. Haiku-poems commonly describe and shed a fresh light on day-to-day situations. They use images and simplicity of language to give an acute awareness of the outside world and a snapshot of a moment in time. This gives a sense of the 'now', a magnifying of the present moment. A haiku embodies brevity and simplicity; language is kept simple to be understandable by all. Haiku-poems typically portray what is experienced through the five or six senses, things that can be seen, heard, smelt, tasted, touched or observed in the external world. Here is a beautiful example that embodies this spirit:

they come out

mountain after mountain . . .

the first mists

Chiyo-ni (1703-1775)

    Traditionally haiku-poems do not aim to examine the emotions of the writer. Yet they can provide a wonderful base and medium in which to reflect on step-by-step, and use to express and acknowledge your feelings. The words that you choose to describe the external world can shed light on your internal state of mind. In your haiku you can describe an external world that symbolises your feelings and any aspect of your reality. You can directly express what you are currently feeling and experiencing in your haiku. The reflection, expression and acknowledgement of your feelings are key steps in being able to face these feelings and any situation that may be causing them. Facing these feelings means that you can challenge them and start to change what you no longer want for yourself or in your life. Typically haiku-poems aim to portray the more positive moments of life. Indeed, your haiku can be an affirmation. You can create your own affirming haiku, describing what you want to feel and situations that you want to experience. However, as a medium through which you can step-by-step reflect on, express, and acknowledge your current feelings and aspects of reality, your haiku may also incorporate the less positive moments of life. This carries the wonderful goal of self-healing and self-development.

Chapter Three – Getting Started

How do I write Haiku?

Haiku are written according to differing rules and in several languages. There is no single right way to write a haiku. It may be advisable to base your haiku on the rules used in your native language. You can then develop your own rules based on what you like from other haiku-poems and how you can best express yourself. Here are eight main rules of the genre to guide you in getting started:

1. **Keep your haiku brief and simple**
2. **Avoid rhyming your haiku**
3. **Write in the present tense**
4. **Keep punctuation to a minimum**
5. **Avoid the use of capital letters and full stops**
6. **Include a *kigo*, a season word**
7. **Have two separate and distinct parts to the haiku and not as a run-on sentence**
8. **Consider a length of three lines, of short, long and short length.**

Using the Eight Main Rules

Let's explore the eight main rules in more detail and see how you can use them in your haiku.

1. Keep your haiku brief and simple

The haiku is characterised by brevity and simplicity. Language and grammar should be kept simple. Alongside this, the spirit of haiku encourages the shedding of a fresh light on everyday situations.

> mountain peace...
>
> in gentle waterfall
>
> cascades of moonlight

Within a peaceful mountain scene the focus is placed on moonlight rather than water cascading through the waterfall. This offers a fresh perspective on a day-to-day situation.

2. Avoid rhyming your haiku

Rhyming is not a characteristic of haiku written in English. In Japanese haiku there is a good possibility that two lines will rhyme because of the use of Japanese vowels within a systematically occurring grammatical structure. In English, however, in order to achieve a rhyme the syntax must be manipulated or particular words must be added. This detracts from the simplicity and the flow of haiku. There is rhythm in haiku; a rhythm or flow that mirrors its meaning. This does not need to be nor necessarily will be in the form of a regular meter. Metrical patterns are discussed in rule 8. Rhythm is an individual creation which will help to convey the meaning of the haiku and which will feel right within its context and essence.

3. Write in the present tense

Writing in the present tense enables your haiku to capture a snapshot in time.

In this haiku the 'now' is captured. All focus is on the present moment:

rainbow flight

in rain-soaked skies

arches of light

The power and harmony of the present moment is emphasised by the beautiful combination of sun, rain and colour.

This next haiku also emphasises the potential inherent in one moment:

grey dawn

in a flurry cherry blossom

covers my path

Beauty can transform one moment in time bringing with it hope and a sense of wonder.

4. Keep punctuation to a minimum

In general, punctuation may be used to separate the two parts of the haiku (this is described in rule 7) in the form of a comma, long dash or ellipsis (three dots at the end of the sentence to show that it is incomplete). The Japanese use 'cutting words' or kireji in the role of punctuation. These cutting words are sounded and indicate a pause such as a comma or dash would in English. This pause is of rhythm and of grammar and is used to separate the two parts of the haiku.

5. Avoid the use of capital letters and full stops

Capital letters are generally not used in haiku nor are full stops.

6. Include a *kigo*, a season word

Each haiku has a seasonal theme and contains a kigo, a season word which shows the season in which it is set. These can be words that reveal a season directly, for example specific weather words or names of flowers, or more indirectly with more abstract associations. Some suggestions are given below. Firstly, here are some examples of the power and beauty of kigo in haiku written by two of the Four Great Masters and other well-known Japanese haiku writers.

Spring

the spring night-
in a dawn of cherry blossoms
it ended

Bashô (1644-1694)

The First Great Master of Haiku

Summer

stillness . . .
in the lake-water's depths
peaks of clouds

Issa (1762-1826)

The Third Great Master of Haiku

Autumn

harvest moon . . .
the dragonfly's wings
motionless

Môen (1649-1729)

Winter

winter moon
a river wind chips away
at the rocks

Chora (1729-1781)

To give you some ideas for your own *kigo* here are some words of both direct and indirect description for each season:

Spring

The young sun, petal, cherry blossom, budding, seedling, sow, tree buds, spring rain, daffodils, bluebells, snowdrops, crocuses, tulips, ripe, life force, the beginning, fertile, birthing pains, dark clouds, drizzle, warm breeze, dancing flowers.

Summer

Shimmering haze, crackling heat, sun kisses, carefree, youth, afterglow, roses, long evenings, stifling, scorching, cloudless sky, abundance, lush green.

Autumn

Gush of wind, russet leaves, cool breeze, harvest, gathering, reaping, apples, pears, blackberries, fallen leaves, moaning wind, striped tree, harvest moon, straw bundles.

Winter

Snowflake, pure, white hills, crisp breath, holly, mistletoe, wild berries, frozen, barren, chill, grey blanket, brooding, bitter, the end, predator, short days, bare, withered, ice, dark nights, cold, falling snow, peace.

7. Have two separate and distinct parts to the haiku and not as a run-on sentence

An important feature of a haiku is that it should have two separate and distinct parts and not read like a run-on sentence. Each part should be separate from the other but mutually enrich understanding. In Japanese haiku, the separation is made grammatically and rhythmically through 'cutting words' or kireji. These kireji are typically a sort of punctuation and may be used in the role of exclamation for emphasis. In other languages, grammar or punctuation may also be used to separate the haiku. For example, you may need to alter verb agreements so that verbs do not necessarily agree with certain nouns, thus avoiding a run-on sentence, or omit prepositions. The punctuation used is generally a comma, long dash or ellipsis (three dots at the end of the sentence to show that it is incomplete). Alternatively, punctuation may be omitted. The cut usually results in either the first or the last line being separated as one part, specifically the lines with short lengths. This separation can help to emphasise, associate or contrast sentences or images. The techniques of emphasis, association or contrast can also be done independently of the cut. Once you develop your own style you may wish to adopt a different length of line and to explore other techniques in your haiku; as well as the techniques of emphasis, association and contrast. Look at this example:

in cobalt skies

floats a perfect cloud...

springtime perfume

The preposition 'of' has been omitted before 'springtime perfume' which avoids a run-on sentence of 'in cobalt skies floats a perfect cloud of springtime perfume'. An ellipsis at the end of the line 'floats a perfect cloud' emphasises the split between the two parts of the haiku. This haiku evokes images of a beautiful day heady with the fragrance of spring.

Try to find the cut in this example:

summer storm

through rising haze

heat crackles

The cut comes between 'summer storm' and the remainder of the haiku. The storm contrasts with the heat

which rises in its aftermath.
Look at this next haiku:

in deepest still near

far the knife pierces

my weeping heart

The cut comes between 'near' and 'far'. There is a contrast between the first two lines, specifically the words 'near' and 'far'. There are moments when she is near and moments when she is far. When far there is a feeling of a knife piercing into the heart. The word 'far' also describes the depth that the knife pierces the weeping heart. The line 'my weeping heart' is also in the style of an exclamation for emphasis.

8. Consider a length of three lines, of short, long and short length

In Japanese a haiku follows a metrical pattern of 5, 7 and 5 syllables within three lines. Syllables are in fact not counted in Japanese but rather poets count 'onji', meaning 'sound symbol'. An 'onji' usually represents a shorter sound than a syllable in English. The counting procedure is different than in English, which often results in more sound units in one word than syllables. Thus, if the 17 syllable pattern is followed in English, the haiku would tend to have a longer duration than a Japanese haiku. A study by William Higginson of Japanese haiku recited by a Japanese actress, and English translations of these same poems recited by an American actress, concluded that an English translation of a Japanese haiku should have between ten and twelve syllables in order to accurately mirror the length of the original. You may wish to strictly adhere to the pattern and amount of syllables in your haiku, or you may wish to explore different patterns and experiment with different amounts of syllables.

Chapter Four – Heal through Haiku

How do I Heal through Haiku?

Haiku is a wonderful medium with which to self-heal. In your life you may experience negative life changes. These could be the death of a loved one, the breakdown of a relationship, divorce, the loss of a job or any other event that gives you feelings of loss and grief. Feelings of loss and grief can tear your world apart. Psychiatrist Elisabeth Kübler-Ross suggests that there are five different stages of grief. An individual may not experience all of these stages but usually at least two and potentially in any order. These stages are:

Denial – 'It can't be happening'.

Anger – 'Why me? It's not fair'.

Bargaining – 'I'll do this if you make this go away'.

Depression – 'I feel so sad. I can't be bothered with anything anymore'.

Acceptance – 'It's going to be O.K'.

Your grief may be so raw at the beginning that you feel that nothing will help. You need to work through this pain. Take small steps and remember that time will help. Haiku is a medium which you can use to help take these steps and to help work through your stages of grief.

This guide offers three techniques for the steps of reflecting upon your feelings, expressing your feelings, and acknowledging your feelings. We will work within a specific framework of dealing with the stages of Denial, Anger and Depression, so as to reach a point of acceptance and change. At any time during your haiku writing you can choose to create an affirming haiku. This type of haiku will give you a boost by focusing your thoughts on the positive.

In addition to the three techniques, haiku in itself can benefit the healing process. The very essence of haiku offers the chance to **focus on the 'now'** and to **appreciate and interact with the beauty and harmony of nature**. This in itself has healing power.

Focus on the 'now'. Appreciate and interact with the beauty and harmony of nature

The spirit of haiku embodies the discovery of the extraordinary in the ordinary and magnifies the present moment. This focus on the extraordinary and the magnifying of the present moment can encourage you to focus on the 'now' and to really observe your external world. The focus on the present can free you from the problems of your past and any worries about your future. The close and snapshot observation gives you the chance to see the positive and the wondrous in your external world, even if you are experiencing difficult times in your internal world. The representation of the natural world through the *kigo* draws you into an interaction with nature and if you look, you will always see an aspect of and harmony. Observing and appreciating this beauty and harmony can encourage you to develop a positive outlook.

spring bursts...

awakening flowers

yawn towards sun

This haiku gives an image of newly-born flowers turning to their place in the glow of the sun. The blossoming of these flowers contributes to the beautiful unfolding of spring.

skyward...

glides on living current

cloud tribe

The journey of a flock of birds is observed in this haiku. This journey is an expression of joy and togetherness.

Create an Affirming Haiku

Give yourself a boost by creating your own affirming haiku. Empower and uplift yourself. Use your haiku to portray what you want to feel and what situations you want to experience. By creating this type of haiku you can affirm and visualise the state of mind and reality that you want. This is a powerful tool for healing and self-development.

How to write the Haiku

Create an affirming haiku by deliberately choosing words and images within a subject matter that is positive and evokes hope and happiness. Describe positive feelings and situations that you want to experience, either directly or less directly.

serenity...

above mountain mists

shimmers of dawn

This haiku portrays peacefulness. Dawn shimmering in a beautiful mountain scene evokes a feeling of calm. Reading the words of this haiku helps the mind imagine and feel this peace. Portraying images such as these helps in developing a positive state of mind.

This next haiku describes a desired situation, one of hope and possibility:

twilight...

a new moon hovers

in darkened skies

This haiku talks of new beginnings, of the positive replacing the negative. The doorway to new possibilities is open.

Three Techniques for your Healing

The three guidelines for techniques are designed to give you a way to reflect upon your feelings, to express these feelings and to acknowledge them with a focus on working through the stages of Denial, Anger and Depression. The case studies below show how haiku has been used in these different ways at different stages of the grief process. Reflection, expression and acknowledgement each constitute a major step forward in your healing. From a place of acknowledgement you can begin to face your feelings and start to identify and change what no longer serves you. You will no doubt develop your own techniques or adapt techniques to suit your needs.

Use these three techniques and others that you yourself develop in your own style. Look for those best suited to you to take control and heal through your own words. You may want to work through your feelings in stages. Spend as much time as you like or need at each stage. First of all, reflect on what your feelings are. Technique one uses free writing. Write your haiku as it flows and then look at the words, images and subject matter that you have chosen and consider what feelings these bring to light. Consider what they reveal about any situation that you are currently experiencing. This may be a technique that you wish to try to work through a stage of Denial. Technique two goes one step further. In this technique you actively express your feelings through symbols. Using symbols is a less direct way of expression and gives physical form to your feelings. This may make them more manageable and easier to be able to describe.

Moreover, you can consider the symbols that you have chosen and reflect on any other feelings that they reveal. You may want to use this technique if you are in the early stages of Anger or Depression; if you are at a point where you feel great difficulty and pain when expressing your feelings or describing your current situation, then using symbols can be especially beneficial. This type of haiku lends itself as a good starting point for discussing what you are feeling and experiencing with others in a less direct way.

The third technique offers a way for you to acknowledge

your feelings. In this technique you name what is causing you pain or difficulty directly. If you are working through the later stages of Anger or Depression you may have reached a point at which you feel ready to express your feelings overtly. This technique offers you a tool to be able to do this in a creative and healing way. You can look at the feelings or situation that you have described and decide what you want to change and how you want to feel. Some situations cannot be changed but you can arrive at point of acceptance. This technique will help you to release those feelings that no longer serve you and to make those changes that you want.

Technique One – Examine your current feelings

If you are in a stage of Denial you may be trying to protect yourself from the emotional enormity of a situation by denying its existence or the characteristics of its existence that would cause you pain and distress. You may be avoiding having to feel certain feelings by denying the existence of what is causing them. In this stage you can use haiku to coax awareness of these feelings into your conscious mind and to identify what your feelings actually are. This technique uses an indirect method and gives you the power to explore what you have written and to interpret for yourself what you are feeling. This technique gives you the ability to reflect on your feelings and to reflect on what may be causing these feelings. Reflection will ease your passage out of Denial.

How to write the Haiku

Write your haiku without unduly concentrating on the words, images and subject matter. By exploring what you describe in your haiku and how you describe it, examine the feelings that are brought to light. Look at your choice of words, images and subject matter. Interpret these and consider that what you have written may be a reflection of what you are feeling and of a situation that has occurred or is occurring.

Barbara has suddenly lost her husband at the age of sixty-eight. They had been married for 44 years. She is numb with shock and disbelief. When she walks in her front door she still expects him to be sitting in his favourite armchair in the sitting room. She cannot yet face the thought of a life without the love of her life.

empty shadows

on his threadbare chair

dust gathers

In this haiku 'empty shadows' stands alone but gives a background of absolute emptiness. This sense of emptiness is reinforced by dust gathering on a once well-used and well-loved chair which now sits empty. There is great loss.

This technique of writing haiku allows you to ask yourself some important questions. What does your haiku reveal about your current state of mind? Have you chosen positive words, images and subject matter or more negative ones? Why have you chosen the words, images and subject matter that you have? What may be at the root of any feelings that come to light in your haiku? Is there a particular situation that may be causing these feelings, or a particular person? Do these feelings make up your sense of self and originate from another time in your life or are they a result of something that has happened more recently? This reflection is a vital first step towards expressing, acknowledging and ultimately facing these feelings and is a key step in the healing process and in bringing about the change that you want.

in empty graveyard

dewy tears fall on stone

winter's solitude

Loneliness and solitude are all around. The memories of love gone by culminate in sorrow and tears.

darkness...
in the silent night sky
whispers of moonlight

A new hope of love breaks through the silence of solitude.

winter's night

the first bud of spring rises

from thawing ground

    There is conflict between the old and the new. The pain of old love freezes the springtime promise of new love. Yet the release of past pain allows new love to blossom.

Technique Two – Express your feelings through symbolism

If you are in a stage of Depression it will help you to express and thus let out your sadness. To keep this weight of feelings bottled inside is detrimental to your well-being. Initially it may be too painful to describe this sadness outright. In this instance using symbolism is beneficial. This allows you to express your feelings in a less direct way. By using symbolism in your haiku, you can both express your feelings and give these feelings a physical form. To do this means that you have already made the first step and have reflected on these feelings. You have control over the symbols that you use and they represent what you wish them to. Your symbols can be as obvious or as subtle as you like. Through your symbols you convey your emotions; this constitutes a key step in the healing process. As well as this you also render your feelings less abstract by giving them a physical form. This physical form may help these feelings become easier to describe and more manageable.

This type of haiku can also help you if you are in an Anger stage. Anger is a natural process in the grief cycle but if bottled inside may become destructive to the self and to others. Through writing this type of haiku you can take a more controlled and reflective approach to voicing your Anger. Your symbols can be a way for you to express your Anger and to explore it. This type of haiku is a good starting point to working through the early stages of both Anger and Depression.

How to write the Haiku

Use symbolism in your haiku to express what you are feeling. Actively choose words, images and a subject matter that symbolise how you are feeling and any situation in which you may find yourself. Give feelings such as anger, sadness, fear, loneliness, happiness and hope a physical form in your haiku through your symbols.

Ian has held the position of Sales Manager for over 15 years. Due to company financial constraints he has been made redundant. At the age of 52 he now finds himself unemployed.

He feels that he has failed the ones he loves. His job as a Sales Manager was a big part of his life and identity; now it is as though he is no longer whole. He is at a loss as to what to do. He feels depressed. He believes that he is not half the ~~man that he used to be.~~

steel anchor

flails in wintry sea...

descent

The 'steel anchor' is a symbol of identity; of someone who is steadfast and reliable. However, the word 'steel' begins to betray an inkling of the coldness and challenge which is to come. The use of the word 'flail' is very descriptive and evokes powerful images of difficulty and distress. The 'wintry sea' is symbolic of circumstances beyond the individual's control. This whole line is akin to drowning; all element of control over what is happening has gone. The last line 'descent' both associates and conflicts with the first line. This emphasises its meaning. In normal circumstances, an anchor must descend to the sea floor in order to provide stability. However, in this haiku the notion of 'descent' is in no way positive. It is a descent into despair and depression. An anchor must also ascend if movement is required. In this light a descent can be seen as preventing movement, evoking images of going down and not being able to come back up.

Stephanie, 26 years old, has been in a relationship with her partner for over eight years. She has invested a lot of herself in their relationship and thought that it would be one for life. Out of the blue Stephanie has discovered that her partner has been cheating on her. The betrayal she feels is overwhelming. Her feelings of anger are indescribable. She feels consumed.

cold fire

sweeps through living shell

hollow dawn

This haiku uses the symbolism of fire to express an all-consuming anger. The description of the fire as 'cold' portrays an image of the utter extreme. The second line 'sweeps through living shell' symbolises the anger flooding the body. 'Living shell' evokes an image of something hollow; dead but yet alive. This echoes the contradiction of feeling as if dead inside but being physically alive. The final line 'hollow dawn' emphasises a feeling of emptiness to the future.

Through this technique you are actively seeking out representations of your feelings. You can use these representations to express what you are feeling without overtly having to describe these feelings. At this stage, overt expression may be too painful. By using symbols you can also further explore your feelings by examining the choices you have made and considering any deeper meanings. This continues the circle of reflection. The physical form you give to your feelings through symbols may render your feelings easier to control and less overwhelming. This expression is a crucial step towards being able to acknowledge your feelings. Your haiku may also provide a good point of departure from which to discuss your situation and feelings with others.

in darkening skies

moonlight dances with the setting sun...

a new dawn marches

This haiku talks about overcoming problems and adversity in relationships. The onset of night represents the disintegration of a relationship. Yet there is hope as the two polar opposites, the sun and the moon, can still come together in harmonious interaction. The haiku ends with a feeling of hope and resolve. The contrast of a new dawn with the darkness serves to emphasise that a new beginning will come.

slowly the season...
the ever ticking time of separation grows
arduous the shoot through stony ground

New love is ready to bud but the inhospitable climate
of separation by time and distance are battling with the
wearying tenacity of its growth.

love's beat

leaks from weary core

flat pulse

    The loss of new love not meant to be sucks music from
the soul.

Technique Three – Acknowledge your feelings

After you have reflected upon your feelings and have expressed these feelings through symbolism, you may feel ready to begin to acknowledge these feelings. If you are in a stage of Depression or Anger, by acknowledging these feelings you are making great steps in working through them. Acknowledging how you feel honours you as an individual, as it gives your feelings the importance that they are due. Acknowledging the existence and degree of intensity of your feelings, or the truth about any aspect of your reality, is a crucial step in being able to face them. In this type of haiku you refer specifically to your feelings. This is a more direct way than using symbolism. It empowers you to take control; to describe exactly how you are feeling; to look at these feelings and to make a decision on how you want to feel and how you want a situation to be. This allows you to release your feelings and to create what you want to feel and what you want to experience. It may be that a situation cannot be changed, for example, a relationship break-up. Although you may not be able to change the situation you can change the way that you feel about it. You can begin to accept the situation and to let go of any feelings that do not serve you.

How to write the Haiku

In your haiku refer explicitly to your feelings. Describe what you are experiencing and reveal and name what is causing you pain or joy. Use words, images and a subject matter that overtly describe these feelings and experiences.

Graham started a new job a year ago. It was the job that he had been waiting for. A couple of months after starting some of his colleagues began to bully him. This continued for months. He felt depressed, ashamed, and his self esteem was low. At first he didn't know where to turn. Each morning the thought of going into work made him sick. He suffered headaches and stomach pains brought on by stress and anxiety. Through a process of reflecting on the situation, expressing and acknowledging how he was feeling Graham came to the decision that the bullying had to stop; that he had just as much right to work where he wanted as those colleagues bullying him. He took control; he took back his power. He put a stop to the bullying.

cold echo

in tightening cage words crush

inwards

This haiku gives a feeling of being trapped, of cruel words reverberating without any respite. These words are causing feelings of constraint and powerlessness. The last line 'inwards' is associated with 'words crush' highlighting how the words are causing these negative feelings inside. The pain that is felt is mental pain. 'Inwards' can also be a sign of hope. It can show that in such a case an individual can look inwards, and there find strength to change what they do not want.

This technique of acknowledging your feelings follows on from the previous two techniques and represents a giant step forward along your path of healing. By acknowledging how you feel you honour yourself; you give your feelings importance. You express your feelings directly and this empowers you to look at these feelings and face them. By facing your feelings or any situation that you are currently experiencing, you can begin a process of review and of releasing the negative and creating your own positive. You can reach a point of acceptance and you can start to put into place the changes that you want.

In this next haiku there is explicit reference to love causing pain. Again, by acknowledging the way that you feel you can face your feelings and resolve to accept a situation that cannot be changed, and change that which can be.

barren dusk

in empty depths

love scowls echo

The line `love scowls echo' is a direct mention of what is causing pain. Love here is repeated disharmony emphasised by a deep sense of emptiness. The line `barren dusk' places the haiku in a context of a bleak and unfruitful situation which is approaching an end.

Here are some ideas of words to overtly express emotions around Love:

heart, pulse, alive, embrace, entwine, touch, merge, joy, warmth, heat, contentment, comfort, melody, heartbeat, growth, roots, clasp, soar, float, heaviness, stone, pain, smash, broken, crush, tear, batter, pierce, weep, wrench, empty, void, abyss, darkness, scowl, weary, lost, chained, caged, shadow, light, hope, rebirth, blossoming, opening, eternal.

beloved eyes
spark waits crouching
twin flame

Worries melt as the heart starts to breathe the sweet air
of souls' love.

Reaching Acceptance, Reaching for Change

When you have reached a point of acceptance and are ready to put into place the changes that you want, your haiku-poems can encourage you to maintain your positive state of mind and resolve. Remind yourself of your power to create in your life.

divine source

springs above eroded hills...

beyond destiny

Above the seemingly insurmountable there lies a divine flow and rhythm to life. There may be events that occur within this flow that we may not be able to change. Yet the line 'beyond destiny' suggests that destiny alone does not dictate our journey, but that we co-create our destiny, and thus take responsibility for our journey.

steady hands

weave breathing colours

soul tapestry

We hold the power to create in our lives; to define our experiences and ourselves. Beyond us there is also a power of creation. Some events in life happen beyond our control. We need to accept such events and with our power change what we can by seeking to transform the negative to the positive.

We have undergone the progression of mastering haiku as a creative expression, to mastering haiku as a creative tool for healing. The form and essence of haiku encourages accessible creative expression with immense healing benefits. Haiku is known for its brevity and simplicity. Its rules are open to flexibility and development of individual style. The essence or spirit of haiku seeks the extraordinary in the ordinary; it encourages a close interaction with nature and focuses on the 'now'. Seeing wonder and beauty in nature and in the ordinary has wonderful healing benefits. A focus on the 'now' permits a release from the worries of the past or the future, and opens you to the possibilities of the present.

We have gone a stage further by actively seeking healing through creating haiku. We have examined three techniques which are designed to aid the passage through Denial, Anger and Depression towards a point of acceptance and change. These techniques provide a tool for you to take hold of your power and heal yourself. The techniques guide you through a step-by-step approach to your healing. By working through the steps of reflecting upon your feelings, expressing your feelings, and acknowledging your feelings, you can heal yourself. At any stage during any of these techniques you can give yourself a powerful boost by creating an affirming haiku. Affirm how you want to feel and what you want to experience. Work through the three techniques at your own pace and experience yourself reaching a point of acceptance and change; a point where you transform the negative into your own positive.

Feel your power to be able to face your feelings and any situation that you are experiencing. Feel your power to release those feelings that impact negatively on your well-being. Feel your power to make the changes that you want for yourself and in your life. Embrace your power to heal yourself through your own words. Heal through haiku.

tangled thoughts
self's own love embrace
release

steady beat
wings to inner smile
pure freedom

Notes

For more information on the five stages of grief please go to: Elisabeth Kübler-Ross (1969) On Death and Dying, Routledge. Elisabeth Kübler-Ross (2005) On Grief and Grieving: Finding the Meaning of Grief through the Five Stages of Loss, Simon & Schuster Ltd.

For more information on William Higginson's haiku study please go to: William J Higginson with Penny Harter (1985) The Haiku Handbook: How to Write, Share and Teach Haiku, Kodansha International Ltd.